THE GLORY

By Ginny Seymour

Cover Illustrators
Tammy C. Dickson
Kevin Beeson

Evensong Publishing

THE GLORY
Copyright © 1991
All rights reserved
Library of Congress TX 3-044-408
Printed in the United States of America
ISBN 0-9718325-1-X

The Glory - Christian Primary II, the second book in the Kingdom series Library of Congress catalog card number TX 3-044-408. No part of this workbook may be used or reproduced in any manner whatsoever without the express written permission of the publisher, except in the case of a brief quotation in a review. All Scriptures are from the Holy Bible, New International Version, copyright 1973,1978, 1984 International Bible Society and are used with the permission of Zondervan Bible Publishers .

TABLE OF CONTENTS

Imagine the Glory - A Word from the Author

The light shines in the darkness,
but the darkness has not understood it.

John 1:5

Imagine the Glory

Step into the realm of heaven. Before you God sits upon His sapphire throne. Brilliant light surrounds God and His throne. This light is like the appearance of a rainbow in the clouds on a rainy day. This light contains the apprearance of the likeness of the Glory of the Lord (Ezekiel 1:25-28).

The throne room of God reveals the Glory of God, and, the Glory is in radiant color. This is a color book to explore His Glory. In this text you will find color boxes and color wheels to extend your understanding of God's Glory. This is the story of how God reveals Himself in the language of His Glory.

I believe that the concepts presented in *The Glory* have applications far beyond this text. All the text presumes to do is to introduce the concept and lay down a foundational base. It does not presume to cover all that could be covered.

I can't claim that I came up with any ideas for *The Glory* nor did I know how to put the information together. All of the ideas outlined were beyond my ability to grasp. The Holy Spirit taught me precept-upon-precept. I scribbled notes, researched, prayed and listened.

It has been a personal journey of twenty years to produce this vision. I don't believe any teaching using color to explain a comprehensive view of the Language of God has ever before been produced. Note that all Scripture reference are from the NIV Study Bible.

Hear: *A voice of one calling in the desert prepare the way for the Lord; make straight in the wilderness a highway for our God. Every valley shall be raised up, every mountain and hill made low; the rough ground shall become level, the rugged places a plain. And the glory of the Lord will be revealed, and all mankind together will see it.*

For the Glory,

Ginny Seymour

Imagine His Glory

Kingdom Language
Introduction

God has a supernatural Kingdom. We gain access to this supernatural Kingdom through relationship with God's only Son, Jesus. Then, we can pray for this supernatural Kingdom to function here on earth, as it functions in heaven. Jesus taught us to pray for the Kingdom to come in this line from the Lord's Prayer: *Thy Kingdom come, Thy will be done on earth as it is in heaven.*

This Kingdom is a Kingdom of abiding in the very presence of God and knowing and following His perfect will. In this Kingdom you find favor with God and His divine destiny for your life.

As with every kingdom, this Kingdom has a language, a native tongue spoken by those who live in the Kingdom. God's ways are higher so the language used in His Kingdom is on a different plane, a much higher plane, than any common, ordinary language known through any earthly realm. It is a language of light.

Christians who desire to abide in the supernatural Kingdom of God will want to know this language God speaks so they can learn to speak it themselves. The purpose of *The Glory* is to familiarize Christians with the language of the Kingdom of God, His language of Light. Let's take a look at the composition of the Kingdom language.

Bible records the first time God speaks in Genesis 1:3. *And God said, "Let there be light," and there was light.* Within that one sentence, God makes known His language of

His Kingdom. God reveals He speaks a language of light; He speaks with an audible voice and His voice produces order.

In the beginning, light was a language not necessarily using words, but truly a language of revelation known all over the earth. Then came the fall of man into the world of darkness. Now we search to know what was the light God spoke?

We know that Jesus calls Himself the Light of the World. He came to earth as the Light of the World. And, He was the Light God spoke to earth at the beginning of time (John 1:4-5). It was His Light that first illuminated the world.

As Christians we acknowledge it is only through coming to know Jesus, the Light of the World, that we emerge from darkness to see the Kingdom of God. As we accept Jesus as our Lord and Savior, we enter God's Kingdom and the eyes of our understanding open.

Jesus is the one, true light. It is through walking in relationship to the true light that we have a revelation of Kingdom language. This light of Jesus then becomes our framework and perspective through which we then view all Kingdom language.

This first recorded sentence God spoke reveals not only light of God, it reveals the voice of God. There was an audible sound at the moment of creation. This voice was the a voice of authority calling into being those things that had not been before.

In the beginning was the Word and the Word was with God and the Word was God. He was with God in the beginning. Through Him all things were made; without Him nothing was made that has been made (John 1:1-3).

Jesus was the Word at the beginning of time. And then, 2000 years later, He comes to earth as the Word. In the New Testament, He expressed this Word as He functioned as King, High Priest and Prophet. He followed the pattern of the Old Testament where the inspired Word of God was spoken or written only by kings, priests and prophets. He was, and still is, our King, high priest and prophet(John 4:14-27,Hebrews 7:1-17, Revelation 7:14).

The third area this Genesis sentence communicates is order. Numbers determine order and relationship. It is through numbers that absolute boundaries are established.

Before God said: *Let there be light (Genesis 1:3),* the world was in chaos, but after He spoke light, the world had form and order. That form and order is reflected through numbers.

When God spoke He literally imprinted the world with Himself. Creation is triune. It is a numerical pattern of order and relationship. Out of God's triune nature He imparted into His creation His triune pattern in the atom, the basic unit of all created substance. God called forth His triune order into nature and into man. These are then the three areas that Genesis 1:3 reveals about Kingdom language. It is light, voice and numbers.

THE LANGUAGE OF SIX

Kingdom language has a base of six. In light there are three colors - colors not made from any other colors. They are primary colors. The primary colors are: yellow, red and blue. Combinations of any two of these primaries form the secondary colors of green, orange and purple. There are a total of six colors. All other colors are made from these colors. White and black are not considered colors.

With voice, it is the voice of king, priest and prophet. These three can be heard through either a voice of concept, or the voice of detail. They are concept king and detail king, concept priest and detail priest and concept prophet and detail prophet. There is a total of six voices.

Although numbers are presented through the base set of 1-9, we consider the numbers 1-6 only for this study. For six days God created. Then He rested. Numbers one through six are the number of creation (Genesis 2:2). Numbers after six are all considered numbers of rest.

Kingdom language is formed with light (six colors), voice (six Kingdom voices), and numbers (numbers 1-6). We will study each area separately and then see how they work to enhance the understanding of each other.

LIGHT CHARTS

Throughout this text an overall-view of the language of God is revealed through light. This light is seen in color. Colors are then displayed on special charts. These charts are simply color wheels, also called color stars. These charts are used as language is first and foremost a product of light , and it is through light that the language of the Kingdom is viewed and understood. The first color star charts light as it is revealed in the three primary colors and the three secondary colors.

The second color star overlays colors with the six voices of prophet, priest and king. The third color star adds numbers one through six. The charts are visuals of the relationship between light, voice and numbers. All representations of the color stars in this text are understood to be representing the light of God's Kingdom.

Each chart is first a graph of light, for it is only through light (color) that the Language of God can be understood. It is only through Kingdom light that we understand what God is speaking, for the native language of God's Kingdom begins in understanding and discerning of God's light. We must be able to discern Kingdom light to know we walk by that light.

Learning to interpret this language will help understand the Kingdom and understand others who live in the Kingdom. If you discern a color, hear a voice or observe order (number), you can learn to recognize what your are hearing.

All begins with light. As you read through the text there are boxes or graphs to color. Coloring reinforces your understanding of Kingdom language.

This study has been designed to exponentially accelerate your knowledge of the language of God's Kingdom.

1

Color - The Glory of God

In the beginning of creation, God created everything. *And God saw all that He made and it was very good* (Genesis 1:31). Before the third day of creation there was only darkness. On the third day of creation God spoke light. Light and color existed before the creation of the sun, moon or stars (Genesis 1:3). This light was perfect. These colors were true. Their reflection was only of God. That light was Jesus.

God spoke and all of His creation was saturated in a prism of color. From Ezekiel we find the understanding of color as the Glory of God. This color that came from the light around His throne is the appearance of the Glory of God.

Like the appearance of a rainbow in the clouds on a rainy day, so was the radiance around Him (God). This was the appearance of the likeness of the Glory of the Lord (Ezekiel 1:28).

This same Glory is mentioned again in Eze. 3:12, Eze. 3:23, Eze. 8:4, Eze. 10:4, Eze. 10:18, Eze. 11:23. God wanted to make it "easy" for man to discover His Glory. His Glory is revealed through color. This glory is His only Son, Jesus!

Hebrews 1:3 states, *The Son is the radiance of God's glory and the exact representation of his being.*

What and who Jesus is can be viewed by studying His Glory by studying color. This book is about His Glory revealed.

Once you learn to recognize the Glory of God you can choose to allow the glory and the light of Jesus to radiate from you. You can choose to stand in the Glory of His Language of Light! It is not our light, nor is it our glory , but rather it is the Glory of the Lord Himself pouring through us.

Let your light so shine before men that they may see your good works and give glory to the Father who is in heaven (Matthew 5:16).

TWO KINGDOMS

In the beginning, God called light into being (Genesis 1:3). Color (though light) came into being at God's command and it was perfect. The reflection was only of God. It was His Glory revealed. God established the pattern. He called man into this pattern. He gave man authority over the earth.

The first man, Adam, hand his authority over to Satan and mankind fell into darkness. Satan can only work within the pattern God already established. Satan is unable to create anything new since he is simply a fallen angel, a created creature Himself. He is not a creator. This fallen creature was handed dominion because of the fall and sin of Adam.

Satan, hating God, did everything he could to destroy the reflection of the Glory of God. He used the pattern to establish a false language, a language of lies, in order to sabotage and to debase in any way God's Language of Light.

God speaks to the differences between the two languages and clearly points out why we need to listen to Him in the following very telling statement from the Gospel of John:

Why is my language not clear to you? Because you

are unable to hear what I say. You belong to your father the devil and want to carry out your father's desire. He was a murderer from the beginning, not holding to the truth, for there is no truth in him. When he speaks he speaks his native language for he is a liar and the father of lies and his native language is lying (John 8:43-44).

Satan is the father of lies. His ways are devious. But his ways do not always have the immediate appearance of evil. He can pose as an angel of light (full of color) and appeal to the mind, will and emotions. We can begin to recognize his light as it is worldly. It touches on the soul of man and offers power (demonic). It is the light of rebellion against God. Satan's light is only darkness disguised as light. His imitation is the dark side. The lie is truly his native language.

So there are two kingdoms. Each kingdom has a language speaking light. One is a language of the Light of Jesus and the other a language of lies. One represents the Glory of God revealing the Kingdom through Jesus, the Light of the World, and the other one represents the false, fallen imitation, speaking the kingdom of this world of darkness and lies.

Some differences are extremely obvious. Some not so obvious. What you want to know is, what spirit is behind the language. Where you would lack understanding, you can ask the Holy Spirit to teach you to discern the differences.

You won't discern everything you see or hear. That would be overwhelming. Rather, you begin to understand with more clarity the divisions between the two languages. And you can learn to speak and act only out of the language of God, the language of His Glory, the language of holiness.

KINGDOM HOLINESS

The following color chart is divided into a positive side (Godly) and a negative side (one of darkness). It presents the true, positive meanings of color as God created color, and the negative as Satan uses color. You will find adjectives and nouns describing both sides of color, offering a picture of the patterns for light and darkness.

Meanings of words used in the color chart are taken from Scripture references, dictionary definitions and extrapolations of words with similar meanings. Not every description can or will be covered in this study. All the study supplies is an overview of the pattern and some examples. You can then pencil in your own examples.

The color chart is presented in Light (of Jesus) and in the lie (darkness) and the pattern appears equal on both sides because they are placed side-by-side. Note that they are not equal, as the Light of Jesus is on an exponentially higher order and plane than the darkness of the lie. God created the order within which darkness must function. Darkness functions on a much lower order. They are placed side-by-side only so we can compare the distinct differences of the two.

All meanings of each color are not listed. The chart simply denotes a strong outline as a tool to recognize the pattern. You may add to the pattern as you gain understanding of the meanings of colors, and the language you are viewing. As you understand color, on the level of reflection, you see that it is holiness that mirrors Godly attitudes.

In some areas of our lives we do not necessarily recognize proper choices. Once you view where the Glory of God can shine forth, you know that is the language you want to reflect. This is standing in holiness. You choose to reflect the Glory of God. It is a matter of free will. It is a matter of consciously choosing Kingdom Language. You can use the chart to help determine where you need to be choosing to speak the language of light. If you are speaking the negatives, it is time for a change.

REVIEW

The introduction considers God's Kingdom language and how we view Kingdom language through light (colors), voice and numbers. We established that this language has a base of six, and determined that it can be viewed on a color chart.

This first chapter reviews six colors that emulate from light, and it shows how colors are the Glory of God. To choose to walk in this Glory is to choose to walk in holiness.

We have also considered that Satan has raised up a false Kingdom that speaks a fallen, lying imitation of the language of God. His imitation functions on an exponentially lower level. We evaluate the differences between these two languages so that we may learn to speak only God's language and reflect only His Glory.

As you begin to look at the following color examples, you open the door of your understanding and peek into God's Glory. So get out those colored pencils. Color your way to a fresh revelation of the language of the Glory of God!

The Light Chart

The Light of Christ has come into the world!
All men must be born again to see the Kingdom of God!

LATCH ON TO THE POSITIVE

The point of entry is Jesus
the only Son of God.
Jesus is the Light of the World,
and to the world. He is the
the Way, the Truth and the Life.

WHITE

It is light and this light is
the light of **Truth.**
Connotations: Goodness,
good values, purity, truth
and conquest, the Church
Connotations: Truth,
the Bride of Christ

ELIMINATE THE NEGATIVE

The point of entry is Satan
the demon of destruction,
the negative, the father
of all lies. His native tongue
is lying. His ways bring
sickness, disease, death

WHITE

The least thought aspect
of light. Literally meaning
the lie. Also pale, lifeless,
conquest, nothing, colorless,
false appearances,
false values, lack of truth,
zero, total lack of substance,
emptiness, delusions, the little
white lie

Positive
YELLOW

Yellow is a primary color.
Yellow signifies **Hope**,
relationship with the Father,
joy, trust, courage,
praise, healing, anointing,
the Kingdom, the Lion
of the tribe of Judah.
Connotations: Honor, pride,
happiness, praise, gold,
hospitality, humility, valor,
gratitude, caution, wisdom,
exuberance for life, judgment,
tithing, integrity, golden rules,
laughter, healing, wealth

Negative
YELLOW

Bitterness, **pride** self-love,
tart like a lemon,
hopelessness, distrust
Connotations: Cowardly,
resentful, ungrateful,
judgmental, insolent,
vanity, vain, full of pride,
yellow journalism,
disease, jaundice, critical,
mocking laughter, spoiled,
self-centered, haughty,
acidic, wealth, harassing,
legalistic, exact law,
dictatorial, gossip

RED

Red is a primary color.
Red means **Love**, blood,
strength, mercy, heart
relationship with Jesus.
Connotations: Redemption,
holy sacrifice, high rank, birth,
warning, righteous indignation,
holiness, intercession, blood
covering, blood covenant,
happiness, encouragement
passion.

RED

The color for **lust, anger,
rebellion,** murder, blood,
evil intents of the heart,
perversion, devil, abuse,
fire, damnation, unbridled
passion, violence, hell.
Connotations: Witchcraft
ill-repute, lust, rebellion,
Communism, porn, rage,
anger, contention,demons

Positive ☐
BLUE

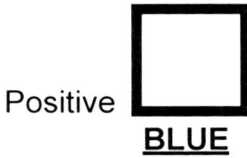

Blue is a primary color, the color for **Faith,** the heavens and the waters, aristocratic, authority, the throne of God, relationship to the Holy Spirit. *Connotations:* Calm, the heavens, water, refreshing, authority, peace, revelation

Negative ☐
BLUE

The color for sadness, **fear,** depression *Connotations:* Cold, cool, feeling blue, melancholy, loneliness, isolation, gloomy, craven fear, paralyzing, faithlessness, emotionless, phobias

☐
ORANGE

Orange is a secondary color and a complement of blue. Warm and sweet. *Connotations:* Calm, placid, unruffled, serene, quiet, peaceful, (see blue), tranquil, agreeable, fragrant - like an orange, full of fire and color, radical, refreshing, undisturbed, cleansing, healing

☐
ORANGE

Secondary color - combination of red and yellow. Loud, demanding, color of Halloween. *Connotations:* Harsh, devastating, maniac, relating to cults, rude, interruptive, contrary, dealing with witchcraft, witches, pride, self-will, obstinate, pig-headed, inflexible, manic, frenzied, hyper

Positive ☐
GREEN

Negative ☐
GREEN

Green is a secondary color and a compliment of red. It stands for the color of the earth. It creates alpha waves in your brain causing calm.
Connotations: Hope, calm, growing, resurrection, direction, new life, spring, boundaries, Savior, refreshing, full of newness of life, nature, all of creation, renewal, maturing, healing rebirth, revitalization

Secondary color - a combination of yellow and blue. Jealousy, envy. *Connotations:* Poison, murder, hoarding, greedy, suspicious, avarice, divisive, rage, anger, destructive, green with envy, spite, coveting, green-eyed monster

☐
PURPLE

☐
PURPLE

Purple is a secondary color, a compliment of yellow. It stands for the royalty of kings and queens and the Church, grace.
Connotations: Royal blood, honor, high office, elaborate, regal, powerful, used in the robes of kings, authority and wealthy, rulers, opulence, affluence, luxury, humility

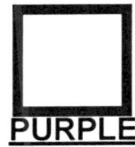

Combination of blue/red It means harlotry, power, the color of mourning, sadness. *Connotations:* Social position, love of the world, moodiness, the despotic church, grief, torment, heaviness, whoredom, power plays, tyrant

Positive

BROWN

Brown is not a primary nor a secondary but rather a tertiary color which comes from the mixing of any two secondaries.
The dust of the earth and dominion - man was formed from the dust of the earth.
Connotations: Man, the life - giving soil of the planet, teeming , fruitful, prolific, fertile, sovereign, to master, plentiful, productive, warm, free

Negative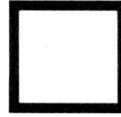

BROWN

Lifeless, sterile, total lack, empty of life, desolation, and dust.
Connotations: Infertility, slavery, bondage, non-productive, not bearing fruit, dusty, dirty, unclean and filthy, something to walk on like dirt, lifeless, being sterile, total lack

BLACK

Black is a mix of colors and where all colors are absorbed.
Connotations: Rich, (being in black means financially successful), warm and enveloping, colors working together, authority. strength, Jesus as the Bridegroom.

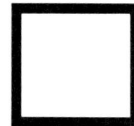

BLACK

Devoid of light, devouring, cheerless, colorless, no light whatsoever, empty, dismal, gloomy, wicked, satanic practices (like black magic), represents the underworld, devours light, tormenting, mourning garments, hole, hopelessness, death.

This is the *verdict: light has come into the world, but men loved darkness instead of light because their deeds were evil. Everyone who loves evil hates the light and will not come into the light for fear that his deeds will be exposed. But whoever lives by the truth comes into the light so that it may be seen plainly what he has done has been done through God (John 3:19-21).*

Therefore if you are of the light choose to walk only in the light. Choose to become light!

BASIC COLOR THEORY

Before we consider the colors on a color chart (color star), let's look at how scientists describe color.

According to physicists, yellow, red and blue are primary colors. Primary colors are colors which cannot be mixed from any existing color. Mixing any two primary colors creates secondary colors. The secondary colors are orange, green or purple. Mixing together any two secondary colors forms tertiary colors creating browns. Color is the visual quality and hue is the name of a color.

Light contains all the colors. White is not considered a color and neither is black. Basic information on color and the Color Wheel (Color Star) is from *COLOR, a Complete Guide for Artists*, by Ralph Fabri, Watson-Guptill Publications.

*Word Studies for the COLOR CHART were compiled from Scripture and extrapolations of words with similar meanings. See pages 65 through 72 for some Scripture references. The Color Star is from: *COLOR - A complete guide for artists,* Ralph Fabri, Used with permission. Watson-Guptill Publications. Copyright 1967 ISBN 0-8230-0700-6 *

The Language of Light ~ Color

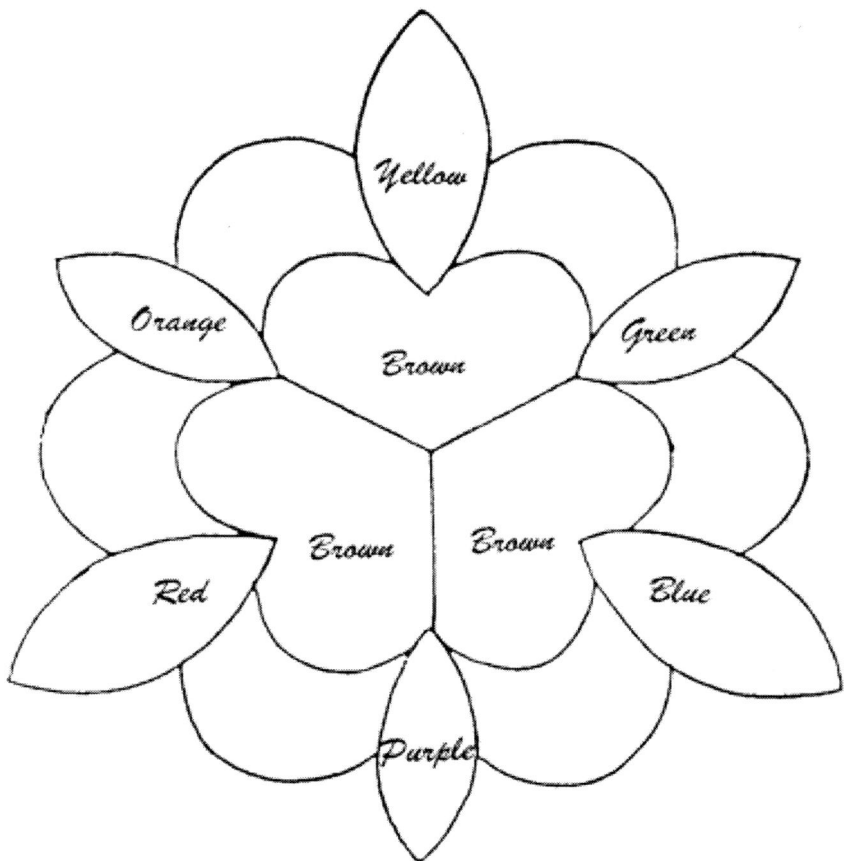

Yellow

Orange

Green

Brown

Brown

Brown

Red

Blue

Purple

OUR COLOR-CODED WORLD

The meaning of colors is an established fact by Biblical scholars, dictionary definitions and psychological studies in many texts other than in this one. The dynamic approach in this study is the dividing of each color from the color wheel into positive and negative categories. The world has clumped all the meanings of a color, whether positive or negative, into one group. Here the colors in the color star have been separated into a positive category labeled good (Godly) values and a negative category labeled negative, worldly or evil values.

God has given us a clue to His creation and it is color-coded. We use this code so unconsciously we are hardly aware it exists; It is so much a part of us, we hardly realize we use the system until someone points it out.

Just living our daily lives we make daily choices in the use of color. We choose one color over another for our car, our homes, the paint on our walls or what color of clothing to wear. We speak in colors: "He sure has shown his colors, the little white lie, I'm feeling blue, she's green with envy, he's a yellow coward, she's a green-eyed monster, he has a yellow stripe up his back, the red-light district, yellow journalism, he's a red neck."

Colors evoke certain responses: People stop for red lights, react fearfully to policemen dressed in blue, give homage to kings and queens dressed in purple and hoard their greenbacks. Even our holidays can reflect the meanings of colors. Take Halloween and Christmas for example. Halloween is a holiday for witches and satanists. The colors are negative orange and negative black. Check out the negative meanings of these colors on the color chart. Christmas, on the other hand, can have a positive meaning: red and green for Savior, hope, redemption, blood covenant and love.

As we are viewing these colors all around us, now we can become aware that they can consistently reflect either positive or negative; either the Kingdom of Light or the kingdom of darkness. Perhaps you never thought in this way before. Christians, using the Holy Spirit's gift of discernment, will be able to tell the difference because Jesus, the Light of the World, lives in them. Therefore they understand light from darkness in ways others cannot.

You already have new applications of ight just by looking at the Light Chart. Here are a couple of examples of other ways you could apply this information.

Has your tongue been critical lately? You can use the Light Chart to check your attitude. Of course everyone should recognize being critical is a negative attitude. See if you can locate this attitude on the chart. You view it as a negative yellow.

If you look to the Light Chart on the positive side of yellow you can see that the opposite of criticism is praise, joy, honor, hospitality and humility. Ask forgiveness for your attitude and start practicing these positive attitudes. It is purely and simply a choice you can make to stand in the light. Positive attitudes reflect the Kingdom Language of the Light and the Glory of God. When you reflect the positive, you are reflecting the light and the Glory of His Kingdom here on earth.

Is your clothing reflecting a negative light? Could you reflect a more positive light? Suppose you choose to wear red. Are you wearing red because you feel rebellious and angry or are you feeling loved and very happy? If you are involved in witchcraft, your red will reflect the negative aspects of red.

How about blue? Do you naturally wear blue because you feel depressed? Or are you full of faith and walking in authority? Now we have a chart that enables us to recognize the difference so we can make a choice or call forth that choice.

At times, God reveals meanings in dreams and visions using color. Colors may be seen in the supernatural and understanding the meanings of color will help interpret what the Spirit speaks. God's Glory can, at times, be seen around people, on people, or appear in pictures, catching a glance into the supernatural. In the supernatural, evil can also be revealed in color. When the color is negative it could appear harsh, ugly, unnerving, overly-bright, dirty, clashing or repelling.

A woman seeks counseling from you. She is wearing a bright yellow that screams at your senses; really annoys you.

Some questions you could ask for the Holy Spirit's discernment: is this person full of bitterness, holding grudges or full of pride? If these are long-term attitudes or attitudes that have been suppressed, healing can take some time. Linger awhile and work on this. Have the patience to persist. Make sure all forgiveness has taken place, even those hidden areas of the heart which only God can reveal. Healing and patience are yellow words.

I have observed the color yellow leave a person's skin tone as they let go of their bitterness and asked forgiveness for themselves and for the one who offended them. Interesting to note that Christians will gravitate towards wearing their color whether they be a voice of the king, priest, or prophet (a topic covered in chapter 2). You can give your ministry away by how you dress, in the colors you choose to wear or colors you like.

The Kingdom we live in is a choice and offers the power to choose and change. Choice is a matter of freewill. Know that having a choice implies responsibility. How can we be light to the world if we do not choose to be a Kingdom light ourselves?

But do consider that a negative color could be discerned but not necessarily mean a negative attitude. The cause could be due to a lack of vitamins, to an illness, to being burnt out, or to chemical imbalances in the body.

Also consider that apparent negative color may need to be handled in a different way. If the attitude is stubborn and resistant perhaps the answer is in inner healing or deliverance.

Another use for the color star: If you discern negative color in a home you can pray using color as a reference guide. Pray for colors to reflect positive meanings. Where before a room might appear dark and dirty in the corners, after prayer, the room will appear brighter, more peaceful and more appealing.

If you close your eyes, when you open them it may seem as if the sun suddenly came out. Everything will appear lighter, cleaner. What are we doing? We are claiming the creation for God and using the color chart as a tool. It is amazing what happens when these prayers are prayed! Always, always, the first place to practice is on your own home and on yourself.

Proceed right down the color chart through the colors that are listed in order. For example, there is more affect on a secondary color if the primaries have been prayed over first. There is more influence on brown when you have prayed for the colors that combine to make up brown.

Here is a prayer example: I had been praying down the color chart. When I arrived at orange I was stumped. All I knew was the negative side of orange and it was all happening in my very own orange kitchen. We could not eat a meal in peace. Loud, rude, contrary, interruptive, hyperactivity and a stomach ache were the menu of the day, served up in generous helpings. I made a diligent search for positive orange.

I prayed, "In the Name of Jesus, this negative orange will have no more influence," and then I listed the negatives. After this, I prayed, "In the Name of Jesus, let this orange kitchen reflect the positive aspects of orange." I then listed the positive attributes of orange.

I could hardly believe my eyes as I watched the change. As further proof of a work being accomplished, the kitchen area quieted down. Later in that week several friends popped in to visit. Their first comments were about my orange kitchen.

"What have you done to your kitchen? It's rather sweet!." Another stated , "I used to hate your orange kitchen, but somehow now I like it."All this happened without me telling my friends about how I was praying.

Here are some other examples of how I prayed. One time I received a lovely Christian wall hanging with a Scripture on it from a friend. But the moment I touched it I realized my friend was furious with me. Now, even though it was from a Christian store and carried a Scripture, the object was hot with her fury. We were good friends and I certainly couldn't just get rid of it. So I prayed over this gift removing the anger (red) and praying that instead of anger, her gift would reflect her love for me. Of course, I also prayed for a healing for our relationship.

Another time I received a carving of an animal from a Christian as a gift. I was stunned when I opened the package. This simple object carried a spirit of witchcraft on it and that witchcraft was aimed towards me. It was a revelation that came every time I looked at or touched the object. And even though it was a white object I could see and feel the red, angry heat of the witchcraft. I prayed to break the curse sent into my home and then, once the curse was broken, I got rid of the gift. I was also alerted to pray that any other gifts of witchcraft being sent my way from this Christian were halted in their tracks.

On a picture of a member of my family I saw great darkness and the heaviness of depression. I placed my hands on the picture and prayed for the depression and darkness to leave. Literally, before my eyes, the picture appeared to lighten.

We already know that inanimate objects can carry blessing, such as a piece of cloth with anointing oil from a holy person. Why should it surprise us that seemingly neutral objects could reflect the Glory of the Lord or the evil of the darkness? What God does, the enemy can only imitate. This was all new territory to me and each time I was surprised by the revelation.

As always, we need the Holy Spirit's guidance as we learn to discern. Your own household would be a place to start. Other areas should only be as the Holy Spirit leads. Just as with the Word, you study and then if the Holy Spirit brings something to your attention, you pray. Jesus did nothing except at His Father's direction - an excellent model for us.

Some objects or things cannot be prayed over for a positive result. Just a few examples are: Buddhas, texts or objects of false religions, objects of witchcraft, anything to do with pornography etc. These items do not belong in a Christian home.

A key word in this teaching would be balance. This Language of Light is a tool, a Kingdom approach to recognizing how to bring the Kingdom of God here on earth. It is a tool to recognize the work of the enemy. You need to learn to use the tool and not let the tool use you or hurt others. In all we do we are to reflect only the Light of Christ and only the values found in His Light.

THE COLOR OF TRINITY

Finally, the issue of the representative colors of the Trinity itself. God the Father is represented by yellow, for hope and goodness. God the Son is red for with his blood He paid for our redemption and the Holy Spirit is represented by blue.

Sometimes you see the Holy Spirit represented by fire. We know that red is a color representing Jesus. So why then is the Holy Spirit revealing red?

Blue (representing the Holy Spirit) is the most transparent of all colors. It is the color of the sky and water. Through it you see all other colors. When we see the Spirit come in fire He is so transparent that all you see is Jesus. The task of the Holy Spirit is to reveal Jesus to us and help us attain a deeper relationship with Jesus and the Father.

REVIEW AND PROJECT

In this chapter, light is shown as the Glory of God through spectacular color. It is through understanding His Glory revealed, that we can discern Kingdom language. We have looked at how color reveals the Glory of God. Color can be seen and the meaning interpreted with the supernatural vision and discernment from the Holy Spirit.

In the text, color is presented as having both positive and negative meanings. Some meanings are obvious. You can learn to recognize and discern the differences between the Glory of God and the lie and apply that information to yourself, your choices, your family, your environment, people you counsel, dreams and visions and inanimate objects.

Positive colors reflect the Glory of God. The Glory of God is on a much higher plane than the imitation of the enemy even though they are represented, in this text, in a table across from one another.

Learning the color meanings and understanding ways that they can be applied will increase the depth of understanding of what the Spirit can and is speaking and doing. Color is a way God speaks. It is His very language of creation; first and foremost it is the pattern He created. It is His Glory visually revealed.

PRACTICAL APPLICATION

There are three ways this understanding can be applied. First, you can choose light. That is, you choose with purpose to reflect only those things which are the Glory of God. You see the two and you make a decision to speak and live in the light, insisting that your mind, will and emotions follow your choices. You can use the chart to help clarify choices.

The second way this information can be used is to change light. Changing light is through prayer. You can pray over your space, inaminate objects, and people. Through your prayers you take the space and exchange darkness for the light of Jesus.

The third way this can be used is in discerning light. You may see and know where the darkness is because you can see the darkness in and through the color it reflects. This provides you with insight on how to pray.

2
Voice - King, Priest, Prophet

Voice is the second area to consider as part of Kingdom language. Into the first man, created in the very image and nature of God, God breathed His very breath of life. Out of Adam then came that very breath of God to speak God's divine and complete purpose for God's creation. This voice that takes dominion is the actual sound of a human voice speaking the dominion God intended.

In the Old Testament (after the fall of Adam) this language to establish Godly dominion on earth was heard through the voices of kings, priests and prophets of God. Kings, priests and prophets were the leaders through which God directed His people. In the New Testament, Jesus established the pattern in that He came as a representation of all three. He came as the King of Kings, our High Priest and the Prophet (Hebrews 7, Luke 4:23).

Jesus spoke as the King and Priest functioning in the anointing of the Melchizedek (Hebrews 5:1-10, Hebrews 7). Melchizedek was King of Salem and High Priest. Jesus was not only King and Priest He is was the Prophet of the Most High

God (Luke 7:16), the Holy One of God that demons were subject to (Luke 4:33-35). Jesus came in fulfillment of all the Old Testament types of ministry of king, priest and prophet.

Jesus came as perfect man (the second Adam) to restore the authority lost by the first man, Adam. In the New Testament Jesus makes this Kingdom voice of authority not just accessible to some, as in the Old Testament pattern, but accessible to all in His New Testament pattern.

This voice is explored as king, priest and prophet, with each voice having two distinct categories. The six types are: detail king and concept king, detail priest and concept priest and detail prophet and concept prophet. The total number of types is six. Six is Biblical number for man and for Jesus.

A RACE STILL BEING RUN

Let's begin by addressing the two different perspectives: concept and detail. Concept people see the overview and detail people see the details. This example could be compared to the Aesop's tale of the race between a hare and a tortoise. The hare was quick and detailed, the tortoise slow and a real dreamer.

Each weighed the other and judged himself the better. Of course we know who won the race. Had they put their minds together, the tortoise with his reasoning skills and the hare with his attention to exactness of detail, they would have fame that would have spread far beyond that one small race.

Life is full of people who are like the tortoise and the hare. They need each other but because of misunderstandings they compete rather than complete one another. The question is, why doesn't everyone think the way you do?

The following study attempts to explain two different perspectives. With new understanding you can choose to end the contention and the competition. You can move into more positive relationships. In the next few pages you will find some practical background and examples on concept and detail that can, perhaps, help you to recognize the very definite divisions of the two kinds of thinking.

MEMOIRS OF A TORTISE

For me, the journey to understanding which basic type I was, began with an ordinary phone call. I was in Seattle and wanted to check in with my family. A very irate mate answered the phone. He had expected a task finished before I left on my trip.

He felt frustrated because I had forgotten. I was also frustrated as I didn't deem such a small task important. Long after the phone call, I struggled with our conversation. Why was this detail so important to my husband and not to me?

Driving home from Seattle, I was sharing one of my many ideas and projects with a fellow passenger. She listened attentively and then commented, "You're a very logical person, Ginny."

"I am?" I was stunned! I always thought of myself as not too bright, especially since I did not always remember details.

"Yes," she affirmed, "You're logical! You can see an idea and are able to organize that idea!"

Later, after dropping off my friend, I continued on my trip home with these apparently unrelated ideas, the phone call from my irate husband and the comment from my friend, rolling around inside my brain.

SLAM! BOOM! The two seemingly unrelated events collided. As I drove home I scribbled frantically in a small notebook. My mind flew through examples and data to support this incubating theory. The headings on my note pad read: Logical and Detail. I felt the Holy Spirit opening my vision to a whole new way of understanding how people think.

Could the logical person be the visionary, the dreamer, the head-in-the-clouds thinker (like me)? Could the detail person be the one concerned with exactness, down-to-earth fine points, (like my husband)? In *Two Perspectives Defined -The Hare and the Tortoise,* these two modes of thinking will be more fully outlined and discussed.

TWO WAYS OF THINKING DEFINED
The Hare and the Tortoise

In my notebook, I scribbled "logical" and "detail" as two distinct ways of thinking. I have since clarified those terms with a more concise expression by using concept (or idea) person and detail person, for both perspectives are logical.

Discovering how your brain works, whether it is concept or detail orientated can indeed set you free. If you are a concept person, you are finally able to recognize why details are more of a struggle for you. A concept brain holds only so many details and then it kicks them out. Concept memory banks can be truly short-term. They do not necessarily hold detail long-term unless the brain considers them very important. The gift of the concept person is to have the vision for the big picture.

The detail person loves exactness and loves to know every little item. And they remember every little item because their brains are programmed to hold detail. The details, to them, are extremely important!

We need both types to complete the picture: the strong, detailed foundation and the large vision. Without both we cannot build. There are various combinations of both types and each one of us will be closer to one than the other. Once you can see and understand your basic type, your understanding will be opened. The light will turn on! You will be more aware that other people/family members/employers/Christians are not trying to purposefully annoy you. Their thinking processes and their priorities just differ from yours. Perhaps you can begin to understand and value those differences. Armed with this new information, you are now capable of turning what was seemingly an opposing viewpoint into a complimentary point of view.

As you read the following list, you may find that you are a mixture of the concept and detail. A concept person may be detailed in areas they like and a detail person can think in concepts. These categories are general categories and will develop firmer boundaries as you move through the text. The consideration now is to determine, generally, whether you are concept or detail orientated. Then that area of concept or detail will be linked to the voice of the king, priest or prophet. If you are married your mate can help you define your gift.

CONCEPT

See/conceive an idea or thought; abstract notion,
Abstract idea from particular instances,
Formulation of something seen, known or imagined,
Reflecting, reasoning, or meditating,
Resolve by analysis,
A probable, systematic view,
Reflect slowly, deliberately, gather, conclude

Summary:
To see overview; make connections to form theories or perspectives

DETAIL

To store details,
Itemizing, concrete, explicit, involved, cataloging,
Exhaustive, thorough, precise, inventory,
To go into particulars, exacting, exact, careful
Meticulous, point-by-point, scrupulous, verbatim,

Summary:
To absorb facts, store facts, organize facts and recall facts

God is a God of overview and concepts. God is a God of meticulous detail. In His image, God created man. God granted the concept part of man vision and the gift of putting together ideas. He created the detail part of man with abilities in all the specifics necessary to fill in the ideas. God called them, one. Man and woman were created as perfect partners. And then, the fall

Ideally, marriage should be each partner holding the other partner up, filling in for the weak areas to make the union strong and complete. However, when a concept person marries a detail person, the two no longer function as one because of the fallen nature of man. They just drive each other nuts! It is the competition of the hare and the tortoise all over again.

Jesus restores the opportunity for man and woman to enter back into that perfect relationship, the relationship Adam and Eve lost. Now man and woman can both walk together before God as one.

How blessed my husband was when I recognized and began to appreciate that his mind works like a computer storing facts. How free I became when he recognized that my mind works in concepts. We could begin building on each other's strength rather than honing in on obvious weaknesses.

DETAIL CHILDREN AND CONCEPT CHILDREN

Now, to the mix of the family, add one child of a concept nature and one child of a detail nature. Finally, a happy family unit, right? More than likely the family is in competition and conflict. The following is a perfect example from my family.

"Who ate all of the ice cream?" I questioned upon opening the freezer and discovering a newly purchased ice cream carton nearly empty.

"I had some." My son replied, thinking he had given a most sufficient reply and no more detail was needed.

His younger sister piped up, "Sam had four scoops and each of his friends had two scoops."

At that point I had to hold my son back from tearing h s sister limb from limb. His perspective...his sister was tattling on him. To my son it was only important that he admitted eating some ice cream. The important issue to my daughter was exactly how much ice cream had been eaten and by whom.

When I began to understand that my son was more concept and my daughter more detail, I could explain to my son. "Your sister is not intentionally trying to annoy you. She is only speaking out of who she is. Details are important to her. Details are not as important to you. You look at the whole picture - some ice cream is gone. However, to your sister, it is important to express the exact amount."

Being able to explain concept and detail thinking to my children relieved a lot of tension between them.

Often my daughter and I would argue over trivial matters. I could not comprehend why, for her, everything had to be so annoyingly exact. Now I can see we were viewing life from entirely different perspectives. She is a detail. I am concept.

It helps a parent to realize that they will tend to favor and maybe even get along better with the child that thinks as they think. Understanding siblings' differences in the thinking process can help build better relationships.

THE OLD ABC'S

The public school system can be a system of teaching details. This statement is not intended to be critical. Details need to be emphasized especially in the lower elementary. But, it is important not to elevate detail thinking to the exclusion of concept. If details are elevated above concepts our world will become very upside-down and perhaps collapse for lack of new concepts. Conversely, concepts should not be elevated above details. If that happens, there are then great ideas but no detail to support those ideas.

We can recognize, however, in a school setting, whether a teacher is concept or detail oriented, and how the student is receiving that information. This applies just as well to the employee/employer relationship or relationships in a family unit.

In a detail environment a detail student will excel. This kind of student thrives on the "busy work" sometimes assigned at school. The concept student may have difficulty memorizing lots of detail or performing objective tests. They will excel in essay tests.

At times a detail teacher and a concept student can misunderstand one another. The concept student can be very stubborn about what they are willing to do, especially an older student. They need more reason or purpose. The concept student can be judged as not accomplishing much if they are measured by the details not accomplished.

The opposite effect is true if the teacher is concept and the student is detail. The student will be filling in details whereas the instructor grades on grasping the concept.

MORE CLUES TO CONCEPT OR DETAIL

There are some more clues for you to consider as you unravel whether you are concept or detail. Are you so heavenly-minded that you are no earthly good? Are you the absent-minded professor type, always full of dreams and forgetting important tasks and dates? Do you have trouble balancing a checkbook? If you hear yourself muttering, "Those picky details," it should give you a clue to your true nature.

Concept people often have difficulty giving enough detail. They will leave out detail to get right to the point. They expect everyone to follow their line of reasoning. Concept people can have tunnel-vision and need time and space to be alone to dream. They dream a lot but are not able to always make their dream come true because of the details.

A detail person can bore their listeners (especially if the listener is a concept) with too many details. They want to be reassured by every detail that the half-baked plan of the concept person will be feasible. They can miss the big picture by over-detailing.

Have you ever heard yourself saying, "Oh, I just love Trivial Pursuit?" You just may be a hare! Yes there are detail and concept games out there and one would appeal to you more because it fits your thinking processes.

Novels can be written from one perspective or the other. Some writers of the Bible are more concept and some more detail. The Book of John is definitely a concept point of view. The Book of Proverbs is definitely detail. Can you see why certain books of the Bible would appeal to you?

If you recognize what you are doing and why, and what others are doing and why, you can be more understanding. If you recognize weak areas, you can adjust. You can forgive those who offend when you recognize that the offense was unintentional.

ONE MORE TIME

So, there are two basic divisions of thinking: concept and detail. Concept people are idea people and tend to see the overview. Detail people tend to see the details. Opposites attract and marry.

Whether a person is concept or detail affects the way they talk, their personal needs, and what they expect. Understanding whether someone is concept or detail can help you relate to their needs. Becoming aware of your thinking process helps you understand and accept yourself as God made you and accept and understand others as God made them.

As mentioned before, there are three Old Testament voices: king, priest, and prophet. Each of these will be viewed from the point of concept and detail. There are concept and detail king-types, concept and detail priest-types and concept and detail prophet-types. Let's take a look at the basic type of of king, priest and prophet and how each thinks.

KING, PRIEST AND PROPHET

There are three ways in the Old Testament God established for His people to speak with the power, anointing and authority of the Holy Spirit. They were through the voice of: king, priest and prophet. Only a few out of all the tribes were selected for this honor. Each one, was individually chosen by God. According to Jewish tradition, some were called and then anointed to be either a king, or a priest, or a prophet. Occasionally there was a prophet who was also priest, but never all three.

The king was chosen by God and anointed with holy oil

as a sign of his position before God and God's people. The priest was called from the tribe of Levi. The Holy Spirit and other prophets schooled the prophet.

God communicated to His people providing leadership, protection, and direction through the voice of the king, priest and prophet. The Old Testament provides types and shadows for the New Testament relationship.

In the New Testament, Jesus became our example-- showing us how to minister and function in the Holy Spirit. *Jesus functioned as the voice of king, priest and prophet. The order of Melchizedek was established prior to the order of the tribe of Levi in the Old Testament.*

Jesus was called king, priest and prophet, after the order of Melchizedek in Hebrews 5:1-10. Jesus spoke in all three voices of the Old Testament. Through Him we are all released to speak in every one of these voices. But first we need to discover in which voice we already speak.

We all speak with one of the three voices: king, priest or prophet. Everyone exhibits both the negative and positive personality traits that accompany their voice as well. Through examining the traits of the Old Testament kings, priests and prophets we can discover our voice and its areas of both weakness and strength.

Read through the following study and note which category you are most like. If you are married, your spouse will be in the same type, whether that is king, priest or prophet. One of you will be the concept and the other the detail of the same voice.

The Holy Spirit will train you in your basic type. Eventually, you will learn to function in all three. Jesus spoke out of all three; Jesus is our model. As with everything, it is a learning process. Once the entire picture is presented then the overview will be placed on a graph.

THE KING

The Old Testament king was the chosen leader of the

nation. He was anointed by God and the prophet to rule. His concern was ruling with justice and wisdom as he cared for those God had given him. He was concerned with the daily needs and protection of his people.

A good king surrounded himself with wealth and servants and his kingdom fared well in war. In fact, everything the godly king did was blessed when he followed the prophets' leadership.

Not so with the ungodly king who abused his power and tried to manipulate God. The ungodly king led the people away from the protection of God and away from God's true prophets. In the Old Testament kings either used Godly authority wisely or controlled harshly.

God's example of a good king is David. David praises and worships God. David dances before God. David is humble of heart. Solomon, David's son, also rules with justice and is given great wealth and wisdom because of his humble heart.

A modern day mark of those who walk in kingship is that they speak of family, healing, prosperity, health and wealth. They are people concerned with the needs of today, and the needs of the physical body.

God has gifted the king-types with creative power in their tongues. They can speak things into being, like healing and blessing. They have an authority to lead and others follow. They can have a great gift of being a servant-type. This is the king model Jesus gave - the servant king.

A primary problem a king-type can have is seeking after the ways of the world. They must be careful to not walk in the ways of the world or to be caught up in worldly ambitions.

They can have a very critical tongue, (as opposed to a tongue of blessing), be judgmental, be skilled in controlling people, (manipulation), and even attempt to control God. They can have a need to be the center of attention. Especially watch the motivation in the area of power and control, wealth or self-worship.

King-types need to learn to control their tongue and their speech in every area, (including being careful in the area of gossip), thereby spreading blessing instead of cursing. They are people can be great wordsmiths. They like words and are very verbal. They are people that others naturally follow. Goodness radiates from them. Often they are in a position to bless others financially. They are usually very family orientated.

THE PRIEST

The priest was the intercessor between God and man. The Old Testament priest was concerned with sin, holiness, care of the sacred writings and in charge of entering non-Jews into the faith.

The modern day priest type is the evangelist and has a heart for bringing people to Christ, intercession, love, a strong desire to go to the mission field to save the unsaved, a desire to preach the Word and enjoys researching the Word or just researching in general. History is often a favorite subject.

God has gifted this person with love for people and salesmanship. Evangelists are God's salesman and have a special gift of persuasion. The evangelist speaks of sin often and wants their listeners to know what sin is and what it is not.

They are concerned with the soul of man and are God's gift to the unsaved. They are full of energy and like to give hugs. Love oozes from this priest-type person. Mercy is important to them and they can wear their heart on their sleeves. Once saved they like being able to quote the Bible and are avid students of the Word. Often they have a great gifting in the area of music.

Their greatest problem can be found in a rebellious nature. Evangelists must also guard themselves carefully in the area of sexual sin (lusts of the flesh) and witchcraft (which is rebellion). They can be drawn away to a love for worldly music and lose their first love - Jesus.

They can be easily side-tracked into sexual sin and rebellion. The spirit of anger and jealousy can ruin their lives and the lives of those around them. They are in charge of marketing the Gospel and have a great gift of salesmanship. Due to their gift of salesmanship they can err on the side of exaggeration.

THE PROPHET

In the Old Testament a budding prophet was entered into a school for prophets or was apprenticed to a prophet to work for him as Elisha did for Elijah. Elisha recognized that Elijah had a mantle for his position and asked to receive that mantle from Elijah. Elijah told Elisha the mantle of anointing was only God's to give.

Elijah did mighty miracles. Such as when he called down fire from heaven for a sacrifice and then had the 700 prophets of Baal destroyed. Elijah topped this feat by out-running Ahab's chariot back to town. It is most interesting to note that so very soon after these great miracles, the great prophet ran in fear for his life because of Jezebel's threat to have him killed.

One of the major gifts of the prophet is deliverance. First they must be delivered out of bondage themselves, in order to hear the voice of God and lead others out of bondage. They also had a gift of foreseeing the future and performing mighty miracles. One of their great weaknesses, however, is fear.

In the Old Testament they were often asked by God to do outwardly foolish things, for example: Hosea marrying a prostitute. They were God's clowns as well as God's living textbook. Have you noticed the increase in popularity of miming and clowning as part of ministry of the Church?

The Old Testament prophet was usually not a popular person with kings or the people. Yet kings approached the prophet to hear the Word of the Lord and to find God-given direction. If the king was ungodly the prophet found little favor and could end up in prison or dead.

Besides not being well received, another area of great difficulty for the prophet was depression. Jonah became depressed when God spared Nivea.

The prophet of today has to be willing to be a fool for God for the prophetic type is God's living sign to His people. He points out the direction for the church. Without the prophet the church can struggle for direction. The prophetic sees the future.

The prophet is given specifically for the saved and to the church.

The prophetic person is very focused on hearing the Voice of the Lord and pointing out the way. They are always concerned with the truth. Everything is black or white. They speak of faith and peace. They are often familiar with suffering. Their eyes are forever in the future. They are usually people that do not have a lot of friends.

A prophet eats the Word of God, incorporating it into their very being. They savor the book of Revelation, like to read about the future and immerse themselves in symbolic meanings. Their greatest adversary is fear and being negative. They can be harsh. Often they are people in great bondage and in need of deliverance for themselves.

THE SIX VOICES

This section combines the king, priest and prophet voices with concept and detail perspectives. This combination reflects six distinctly different voices. These voices can be heard when you listen to the way people speak.

You will find each voice placed in order followed by definitions. Color boxes are included for you to color as color is used to define relationship which is- the soul, the nature and the emotion of each voice.

THE VOICE OF THE KING

KING Detail  **Color-Yellow**

Positive: Power in tongue to create, speak positively. Can speak things into being. In charge of wisdom, praise and worship, prosperity, funds, teaching and numbers (in a financial sense). They are to serve. Goodness exudes from them. Very verbal wordsmith, and are the most detailed of all personalities. They are gifted in physical healing.

Negative: Can have a very sharp, critical tongue. can be harsh, judgmental, authoritarian, centered in self, into lots of wealth, being overly legalistic, easily distracted by the world and by what the world offers. Can be very controlling.

Can be a Gossip, breaker of confidences, concerned with good looks, beautiful bodies, over indulgence. Can want to detail others into expectations they cannot live up to. Need patience.Can be drawn into worldly ways or worldly philosophies.

KING Concept  **Color-Purple**

Positive: Same as above, however, more into concept thinking. Sees both priest and prophetic views and functions in both. They have the heart of a servant, very people and very family oriented They want to know people are being cared for. Relationships and the maintaining of relationships is very important to them.

Negative: Into power plays and controlling others. Can be opinionated, melancholy, grasping for power, manipulative. Must watch critical and judgmental nature.

Rebellion and fear can be problems. See the above list under detail. Can easily fall into love of the world, harlotry. Can have a fasination with philosophies and their own mental reasoning.

THE VOICE OF THE PRIEST

PRIEST Concept  **Color-Red**

Positive: Loves to research, big-hearted, outgoing, has a love for people and wants to know they are saved. Likes to evangelize, is caring, generous. Can wear heart on their sleeve, is an intercessor and gifted with salesmanship. Likes to be involved in mission work - a heart for the unsaved. Lots of energy. Feelings, emotions, mercy are important. Loves to have lots of friends, emotional, gifted in music, very passionate.

Negative: A rebellious nature is their greatest enemy. They can cause division, be involved in witchcraft or sexual sin, physical abuse and have extreme anger issues or victim or martyr issues. They can cause envy and strife. Unfaithful in any covenant and/or marriage. They can use their power to convince for the purposes of manipulation. They pass blame to others for their sin. Can be overly emotional and then use emotions to manipulate. They tends towards exaggeration.

PRIEST Detail [ ] **Color-Green**

Positive: They offer out hope, comfort, concern and are very dedicated in what they do. They wear their heart on their sleeve as they are mercy people. Can see the prophetic and kingship. Review list above. Full of fun and adventure. Interested in missionary and missions. Have the gift of marketing.

Negative: Jealously and/or greed can be big problem. Can be verbally/ physically abusive and controlling. Causing divisiveness. Unmerciful, unresolved anger issues and overly emotional, involved in sexual sin. Can sell themselves as living a Christian life even if they continue in sexual sin and rebellion.

THE VOICE OF THE PROPHET

PROPHET Concept [ ] **Color-Blue**

Positive: Sees future, gift is prophetic. Eats the Word. Speaks of truth, faith, peace, deliverance. Is familiar with suffering. Loves symbolic meanings. Truth is very black or white. For them, there are no shades of gray. Loves the color blue. Likes cool colors. Speaks with authority. They are a living testament - an oracle of God. They act out the prophetic for the church. They infuse the church with drama and new vision.

Negative: Can be very negative. Fear/ depression are their greatest adversaries. Other problems can be insanity, hearing or correctly hearing or receiving the Word of the Lord. Problems with actually hearing, stubbornness, real learning disorders, backwards reading of letters or numbers. Can be overly introverted and in need of deliverance.

PROPHET Detail ☐ **Color-Orange**

Positive: Traits similar to the ones above. Energetic, very colorful person. Overflow with color and creative energy.

Negative: Can be very negative, fear and depression greatest adversaries. Another problem can be insanity and nervous breakdowns. A lack of ability to hear and convey the Word of the Lord. Their sense of color can clash harshly with difficulty choosing colors that work together. Can be contrary, negative, have problems with backwards thinking and some learning disorders, be overly extroverted, lack listening skills.

KINGDOM VOICE

The audible sound of the Kingdom language is understood by realizing that it is spoken with three different voices. They are: king, priest and prophet. Each one is very different from the other but all are equally important. Each one has a different sound, flavor and purpose.

In our current society, each type is often functioning as an individual identity. You can see it happening in the church. You can see it happening among individual Christians.

Individuals can speak from their perspective and at times can very thoroughly misunderstand one another. It is because their voice (or type) is so much a part of them. They understand themselves but do not necessarily understand others.

Prophetic people may not be happy or accepted in a king-type church. They want a church speaking revelation, prophecies, deliverance - a church that conveys faith and truth.

King churches desire to impart prospering as your soul prospers, tithing, speaking your needs. Priest-types evangelize.

Truly what is being spoken is three distinct dialogues. Together they are the language of one God but from different perspectives. One language is of the king, one is of the evangelist (priest) and one is of the prophet. They sound different because they are different. The good news is that one day all will be recognized and come together and function as one: king, priest and prophet.

Most often people will gravitate towards a church that shares the message in a language familiar to them. What can happen then, is, people in a church might speak one language. They can begin to think it is the only language and therefore the most important language.

You find churches that speak from their perspective saying, "This is God's most important message and we are the only ones who know it."

There have been times in history when one or the other was more acceptable. We have had a heart for missions in the past, but such little current outreach for souls. The focus now is more on a movement with a king-type agenda. The king agenda is very appealing. Who can deny a desire for material goods in this materialistic society? Current society has been in the vortex of humanistic teaching. Sometimes the line between true kingship with its prosperity teaching has blurred into narcissism.

The true language of kings in God's Kingdom is to have the heart of the servant, to give and to be a blessing and to know that larger provision comes with greater responsibility. It is to care for people and their needs knowing that our provision comes from God and is for the support of the ministries not the opportunity for over-indulgence.

Prophetic language has come to the forefront. The problem is it has come as a separate movement and is forced to function mostly outside of the church. The prophetic is given specifically by God for the saved. It is the voice of the prophetic to give direction as spoken by the Holy Spirit. It is for the church to follow. But rather than hearing God is raising up many to speak with a prophetic voice, only a few are being received.

Kingdom magic happens when we function together as one. We release the power to bring in the unsaved, help them, teach them and deliver them. We truly become kings, priests and prophets of God.

Note that the voices of king, priest and prophet are different than the five-fold ministry gifts from Ephesians 4:13. You are first king, priest or prophet and then function in ministry gifts of: apostle, the office of the prophet, evangelist, pastor, and/or teacher. Christians are anointed and then set, by God, within the ministry gifts to serve the body of Christ.

REVIEW AND PROJECT

The first section of chapter two introduces concept and detail. The second section covers the Old Testament and New Testament types of king, priest and prophet. The anointing of God is the concept and detail working within the king, priest and prophet. Viewed as a unit, this is where the true church needs to be functioning - in all three. The three are to be one.Out of the belly of king, priest and prophet comes the voice of God. People will gravitate towards the colors they minister in.

On the following color star is placed the three Kingdom voices of king, priest and prophet.

The Language of Light ~ Color and Voice

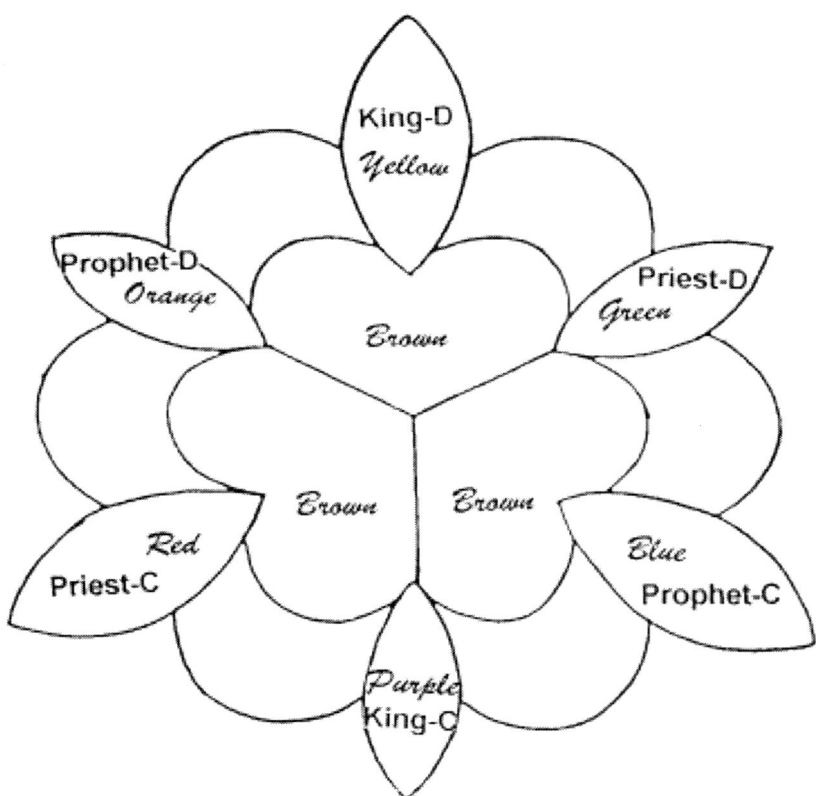

King-D
Yellow

Prophet-D
Orange

Priest-D
Green

Brown

Brown Brown

Red
Priest-C

Blue
Prophet-C

Purple
King-C

3

Numbers ~ The Alphabet of God

Numbers are the language God speaks and the third area we will consider as part of Kingdom language. As Galileo stated so adroitly, "Numbers are the alphabet with which God has written the Universe."

In the beginning the earth was formless and chaotic. God spoke light into the formlessness. Triune God called creation into being. He called it into being in the image of Himself. The image is in the atom. The atom is the triune building block of all of created matter: from rocks, to water, to fish, to all living creatures and to man (the first Adam). Three is the Creator's unit of creation, the numerical alphabet that has written the pattern for the universe.

God spoke numbers and built from this foundation creation. Out of His being, God called into His pattern, numbers. For six days He summoned them. He called them "good." These numbers of creation are one through six, the number of days in creation.

God spoke to His living numbers and commanded, "Multiply! Increase!" He created in orderly fashion and created everything in relationship.

Then God rested; so numbers after six are considered (along with all their other meanings) as numbers of rest. The world was created in six days and man was created on the sixth day. The Biblical number for creation and for man and for the second Adam (Jesus) is the number six. Jesus came as the second Adam to restore that perfect order that was lost by the first Adam.

And so, six numbers are used in this study as a base. However, numbers are defined up through the base set of ten. Ten is the beginning of a new set.

Numbers reflect the Glory of God's perfect order. All God's numbers are holy and express dominion and order. After the fall, Satan could only work within the pattern God created, and so a positive and negative exists with numbers as with color. The goal is to stay on the positive side reflecting God's perfect order.

God is a God of multiplication and addition. God is a God of increase. When God subtracts it is only to add more. The only example of subtraction or division before the fall of Adam was when God subtracted the rib from man to make woman, but God calls man and woman one flesh. God subtracted and then called it one. He made one more than it was before. God enlarged one. Only after the fall did subtraction or division carry a negative meaning.

Note that, just like colors, negative and positive meanings of numbers are presented as being on an equal plane to show how the enemy can only use the pattern God already established. Recognize that just like positive colors, positive numbers are far, far above and rule over the negative because they reveal the Kingdom of God and God's Kingdom is high above all other kingdoms.

THE **NUMBERS** CHART

Light

POSITIVE + *Perfect order*	NEGATIVE - *Fallen order*

0 Before anything,
God was

Nothing at all, void,
zero, totally empty

yellow

1 Holy

Being number 1

being one with God,
God calls Himself
the Holy One, sufficient

being the only one,
self-perfection, humanism
self-sufficiency, self- centered

red

2 Covenant, Marriage,

Division, broken contract,

two becomes one.
Jesus and Father are one,
Old and New Testament

first number of division,
division…Subtraction

blue and orange

3 Father, Son, Holy Spirit,

Powers, principalities,

together they are one,
trinity, yellow/red/ blue,
atom as basic unit of
creation, triune, family

rulers in high places,
end time evil army, 3 negative
primaries yellow/red/blue,
(Revelation 9:17 NIV)

green

4 North, east, west, south,

The world, the bar,

boundaries, the Cross,
Gospels, earth, the world

lack of boundaries,
worldliness

purple

5 Grace, government:

Manipulation, controlling

apostle/prophet/evangelist,
pastor, teacher, Hand of God

hand of man, worldly ways

brown

6 Dominion, language, creation ⬜ The number of fallen man,
number for Jesus as man,   the number for Satan
Number for Adam, colors

     Numbers one, two and three represent the Kingdom. The book, *The Kingdom* has a base of three. Numbers one through six represent Kingdom language. *The Glory* is based on one through six, the numbers of days in creation. After six all numbers are numbers of rest. Nine is the number for deliverance and 10 is the number for a new set.

7 Perfection, harmony,   Disunity, split, divorce
rest, unity, 7 churches,   unrest
7 candlesticks, 7 spirits
of Revelation

8 New beginnings, infinity,   No beginning,
alpha and omega   no end.

9 The power of the Holy Spirit -   The power of Satan,
nine fruits, nine spiritual gifts,   Goliath was over 9 feet
nine areas of deliverance,   feet tall, nine areas of
nine planets - solar system   demonic activity

10 Number for covering the   multiplication of
world, Multiplication   negative

     Number studies are from Scripture references, known understandings in society and extrapolations. God establishes the base set of zero through nine. All numbers above nine are part of a new set. God created the system, and owns the system.

One   THE POWER OF EXISTING IN GOD

When God created man, man was one with God. Adam thought of doing nothing out of the will of the Father. Man walked in perfect relationship with God. There was a oneness before the fall…a living and breathing as one. After the fall, man became centered in self rather than centered in God.

When man is centered in God, man lives in power, authority, knowledge, love, faith, hope and wisdom far beyond his own. Man surrounds himself with these attributes as he surrounds himself in the presence of God. Not only does man live in relationship with God but he lives in relationship with other Christians who move in God. They are all part of the inseparable one.

In the New Testament it is referred to as the body of Christ and we are all parts of that body (1 Corinthians 12). Jesus prayed that we would all be one as He and the Father are one (John 17:9-11).

When God spoke to the people in the Old Testament they asked Him who He was and He responded "I Am". If man does not exist in the God of the "I Am" then man sets himself up as the "I Am." When man is centered in self he separates himself from God. In his own eyes, man becomes the big number one and the source of all wisdom and knowledge and man walks in humanism.

Existing as one with God is the positive way God created for us to exist. Only then do we have intimate fellowship with God. Existing as individuals, separate and independent, poising ourselves as the big number one, is the negative of one. Often the world will have movies or books which have a character who is the only and chosen one to save the world. In God's scheme of things we all are the "one", the *one* that will bring deliverance or healing. We are all the called and chosen *one*.

God has a special relationship with the number one.

He is called the Holy One (John 6:69) and it is the only number referred to with the adjective of holy. One is holy because it is all inclusive. All God's numbers are part of the divine one, His whole unit. They are inseparable.

All of His numbers are part of the one: Man and woman are one, Jesus and the Father are one, triune God is one God, there is only one body. The opposite is the position of Humanism that we are the center of it all - the all-important and individual only one.

Two THE POWER OF COVENANT

In God's numerical system two equals one: The Father and Jesus are one (John 17:20).Husband and wife become one in Genesis 2:24. The Old and New Testament equals one. There is no room for division as the two become an inseparable covenant of one. This is the kind of covenant a Christian comes under when they ask Jesus into their heart - a covenant where Christians are bound to Jesus as one.

Three THE POWER OF TRINITY

God is a God of trinity, a triune God. God created a universe in trinity. Out of nine planets he chose the third planet from the sun for His creation. Even the smallest unit of creation, the atom, is three parts: proton, electron, and neutron. As a created creature of God, we are three parts: body, soul, and spirit. God has a signature number and that number is three.

Two other trinities observed within this text are, primary yellow, primary red, and primary blue. The anointing is: kingship, priest, and prophet. There are other threes as well: the Trinity: time (past, present, and future), and the arts (art, music and drama). All these can be placed first on individual triangles. They can also be placed over the top of each other, for they literally overlap and explain each other.

God

Father

Son △ Holy Spirit

Kingdom Pillars

Hope

Love △ Faith

Light/Colors

Yellow

Red △ Blue

Numbers

1

2 △ 3

Kingdom Ministry

King

Priest △ Prophet

Man

Body

Soul △ Spirit

Time

Present

Past △ Future

The Arts

Art

Music △ Drama

Read all top points of each traingle as a group. This group is reflected in the ministry of the king type. All left points reflect the ministry of the priest. All right points reveal prophetic ministry.

The Power of Created Form

In Geometry nothing exists until you have three points. There are no complete figures representing one and two. No form with one point. With two points you can draw a line. But, when you have three points, you have the first form.

God spoke, imparting into the atom His divine order, His triune nature of three. So, the first shape to have form is the triangle. After three, many other forms follow. Three is the language of created substance.

Four THE POWER OF BOUNDARIES

The four in a positive sense, would represent boundaries in each of the four corners of the world: north, east, south and west. It also represents the four seasons, the four Gospels (Ezekiel 1:5 footnote NIV), having boundaries, the world. Four is used forty times in the Book of Ezekiel.

FOUR ~ The Language of the World

As three is the number to represent the language of God, I believe that four is the symbol for the language of the world. It is represented by a bar (or rectangle). Through the worldly language Satan speaks to three areas: physical/material, soulish (rebellion and witchcraft) and the spiritual. Along with that, he speaks opposites or we could say he speaks out of both sides of his mouth, or that he speaks with a forked tongue.

In the physical, Satan speaks the language of the philosopher, a language rooted in Greek philosophy. The first language He speaks is about the physical, being number one, being self-centered. The number one speaks of being centered on wealth for yourself or the opposite, to be a kind person giving away your money to good causes. It speaks worship your beautiful body (or other beautiful bodies) in physical appearances or in athletics or to hate your body because it is not perfect (or to be overly concerned with the care of your body).

It speaks the language of Humanism: personal rights over boundaries established by God, and elevating human law higher than the Law of God. It elevates self-worship as a way of life, narcissism in the fullest sense, political correctness. It is all about worship - self or other. Or lack of worship-atheism.

The second area Satan speaks is rebellion and perversion. Live it your way! Or pervert the Gospel and pervert love simply to being sex, and man simply a sexual creature. Satan preaches a platform of porn through visual (TV/magazines/

video games/bars) and audio (music/TV programs). He speaks to the soulish nature of man. Witchcraft for evil or for good (white witchcraft). He speaks divorce to tear apart home and children, the right to abort, the right to divorce, the right of homosexuals, the right of same sex marriage. It's all about the right to choose evil over good.

The third area Satan speaks is in the spiritual realm. He speaks personal power through forbidden knowledge. He tries to sell the idea that his power is so much greater than God's. He uses video games, movies, television, educational institutions and cartoons to preach magic, mythology, spirit guides and false religions. The results are fears, phobias, depression, oppression and possession.

Five THE HAND OF GOD

The positive number five represents the hand of God, the anointing of healing and the seal of the king. An example of that anointing would be Joseph. The sun, moon and the stars bowed down to him. His coat of many colors was the glory God gave to him. Five is also for grace, government, and authority.

Six COLORS, NUMBERS AND MINISTRY

Six is the number for man and creation. On the sixth day man was created out of the dust of the earth. Six is the number for the color and voice and the Language of God.

Seven THE POWER OF PERFECTION

Seven is three and four, in geometry this is a triangle and a square. It represents harmony and peace. The Book of Revelation uses the number seven 52 times. It is the number for completeness. Seven is the number for rest for in six days God created. On the seventh day He rested (stopped working).

Eight THE POWER OF NEW BEGINNINGS

The number eight could be represented by the figure eight laying on its side. Eight represents the never-ending new beginnings. God is the Alpha and Omega. He is the God of new beginnings.

Nine THE HOLY SPIRIT

Whenever God speaks, all three persons of the Trinity are present and they will always agree with each other. This is illustrated in the picture below.

Father God speaks and Jesus and the Holy Spirit confirms.

FATHER

JESUS △ HOLY SPIRIT

Whenever God the Son speaks all three persons of the Trinity are present. the Father and the Holy Spirit will have input on the issue to clarify and confirm what the Son speaks.

FATHER

JESUS △ HOLY SPIRIT

Whenever the Holy Spirit speaks all three persons of the Trinity are present. The Father and the Son will have input. They confirm what the Spirit is speaking.

FATHER

JESUS △ **HOLY SPIRIT**

Nine reveals completely every way God speaks and every way He confirms.

THE FANTASTIC NUMBER Nine

The number nine is the only number that no matter what you multiply it by the sum product added together always adds down to a 9.

EXAMPLE 1   9 x 7 = 63
Add the two numbers of the sum total together.
6 + 3 = 9

EXAMPLE 2   9 X 56 = 504
Add 5 and 0 and 4 together.
5 + 0 + 4 = 9

EXAMPLE 3   9 x 362 = 3258
Add three, two, five and eight together.
3 + 2 + 5 + 8 =18
Now add one and eight together.
I + 8 = 9
Try any number. It always works.

NUMBERS TEN AND ABOVE

Ten THE POWER OF OWNING THE WORLD

The number ten is the number for multiplication. Through the tithe of ten percent, God promises to rebuke the destroyer and multiply back to us.

The story of the mustard seed and the tree that grows from it is also an example of the number ten. The mustard seed eventually grows to the height of ten feet. The significance of the height of ten is that ten is the number for owning the world.

The symbol X stands for ten and also multiplication. The symbol X also stands for the taw, the last letter of the Hebrew alphabet. In Revelation 7:2 9 (see footnotes) it states that there will come a people at the end of time that God will mark with His

X, His taw. Presently there is a generation of youth growing up that is called Generation X. The world says that they have no hope. However, in God's number system they are a generation marked for Him. They are a generation that can own the world.

NUMBERS ABOVE TEN

Concerning God's numbers, when God expresses a number above the base I believe that it takes some of its meaning from actual face value of the number in the base set. Numbers higher than nine can derive their meaning from the actual meaning of the number as well as the multiplication or addition of their combined numbers.

God not only owns numbers through multiplication and addition, God owns numbers both forwards and backwards. It is interesting to note that language is expressed reading from left-to-right in some cultures and reading right-to-left in other cultures. One is a more western form of reading and thought, the other is an eastern form of reading and thought.

An example of a number being read both ways is the number thirteen. Thirteen has long been considered a negative number carrying a negative meaning such as a curse, superstition. In fact, in our current society it is difficult to think of a positive meaning for the number thirteen as it is used primarily as a negative number. The left-to-right reading of thirteen is based in superstition and curses. The right-to-left reading would be thirty-one. Thirty-one negative is used for the witches' holiday of Halloween.

From the study of numbers we know that all numbers have a positive meaning for God created them and owned them first, backwards and forwards. God owns this number thirteen and it's time the church realized it and take back what is rightfully theirs. God owns thirteen left-to-right and right-to-left.

There are thirteen months in a Jewish Calendar (perfect order). In a Jewish calendar you can tell the time of the month by looking at the evening sky. You always know what day it is by simply looking at the night sky.

Thirteen is the number for Jesus and twelve disciples (perfect number of relationship). It is found in faith, the Mustard Seed 13:13, It is found in the Book of Hebrews as this book is 13 chapters long. It is found in love: 1 Corinthians13 and Jeremiah 31:3. It is found in hope, Proverbs ends 31:31, the Proverbs woman is Proverbs 31, and number for warfare on Military clock is 13. It is Genesis1:3. It is the number of one God in His triune nature. Thirteen and thirty-one are numbers that reveal God nature. You could see why the enemy would want to debase their meaning and only have people see them as nevgative numbers.

Just one more thought before leaving numbers. Our system of numbers goes back to a Roman base. God has a base of three, first in His triune nature of creation and as triune God, then in this text as six (the number for man and for Jesus), and nine, the number expressing the Holy Spirit in the text, Christian *Primary III, The Power.*

Perhaps in our western thinking, we have missed a whole way of understanding numbers. Perhaps there is a pattern of mathematics more accurate using a base of three that we are not accessing. Obviously, it is a language God Himself developed and would seem to recommend.

PLACING NUMBERS ON THE COLOR STAR

We know that yellow is one, red is two and blue is three. The secondarys are a combination of the primaries. So orange would be three because it is a combination of yellow (1) and red (2). Purple would be five as it is a combination of red (2) and Blue (3) and green would be four as it is a combination of blue (3) and yellow (1).

Numerically the primary and its' complimentary added together is 6. So yellow and the compliment purple is 6. Red and the compliment green is 6. Blue and the compliment orange is 6. Six is represented by the browns. The number for man is six. Man was taken out of the dust of the earth.

Language of Light ~ Color, Voice, Number

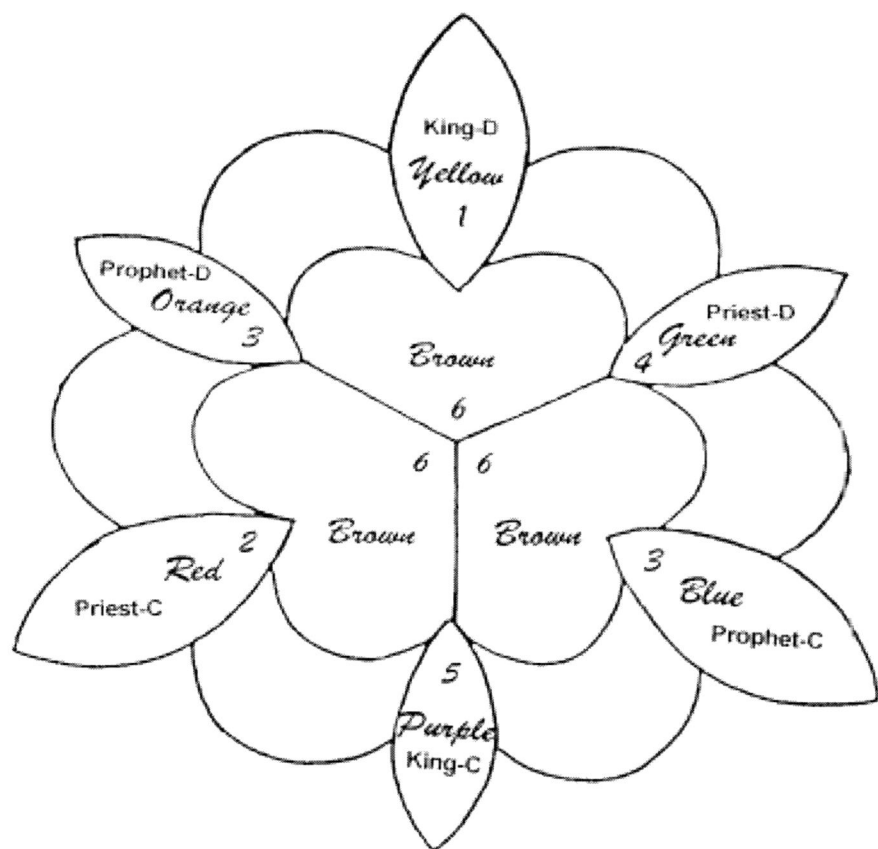

King-D
Yellow
1

Prophet-D
Orange
3

Priest-D
Green
4

Brown
6

6   6

Brown

Brown

Priest-C
Red
2

Prophet-C
Blue
3

5
Purple
King-C

REVIEW AND PROJECT

Numbers speak of the Glory of God. They are the Language of God spoken forth at creation. This positive, numerical language brings forth relationship, blessing, increase, form and substance, absolute values and order out of chaos.

God created man to walk in the order and relationship of these physical boundaries. Numbers carry physical boundaries we can choose to acquire. God will use this numerical language to add and multiply to us. When He subtracts it will only be to add more.

Numbers can be used in a negative sense. Negative meanings of numbers is a usage by the enemy. It is up to us to understand the positive meanings and walk in the order and relationship of positive Godly order.

4
Relationships

In relationships people can work out of negative order. Below are some examples of negative order being acted out through relationships.

There are games in relationships. Games that keep people in an endless rat maze, with a repeating continuum of negative results. The same game is played over and over. The games are all about power and control and are always in a "no win" situation. The only way to get out of the game is to recognize it and stop playing. Below are examples of negative games.

THE GAMES PEOPLE PLAY

The lie is the source of all of the games. It is the prism under which they are played. There is no moral constant and no fairness. The games are mean. There are no rules.

1 THE SPACE GAME

I am number one. I own the space and you need to be out of my space. It can be played as a control or anger game. One person demands to place their needs constantly above the needs of the others. When you enter a room you can feel strongly that you are not wanted in that room by a person in that room.

You can not allow the selfishness for the first game. For the second game you can command the power be broken and no judgment or anger come against you.

2 THE VICTIM GAME

This is a game of verbal or physical abuse. When a victim receives abuse, the abuser finds fault in the victim accusing them of a shortcoming that deserves abuse. The abuser always finds fault with the victim. The victim accepts blame because they believe they are guilty and deserve the punishment they receive. Sometimes people accept abuse as they take on the role of a martyr.

Victims may have come from an abused family or have a poor concept of themselves. The abuser demands perfection so there is always room for punishment. The abuser can be very apologetic and even nice. However, this is only a ruse and the cycle repeats. This game has to be called by name, faced down and stopped. It can lead to murder. If alcohol or drugs are added it becomes even more random and dangerous.

3 THE GAME OF FEAR

Subtle threats to allow a person to know they are out of favor usually with actions or threats of violence. Anything to place fear in a person so they will conform, be afraid to leave or be afraid to act.

4 THE BABY GAME

This is a game of a lack of boundaries. The baby game is often played by children, but sometimes played by adults who have not grown up with boundaries to their behavior. Some responses to the lack of responsibility could be: "I didn't know the rules, so I'm not accountable. Were there rules? I forgot there were rules. I didn't understand the rules. That's not the way everyone else does it. All other kids/ people do it/did it this way. I always get the blame." (This is called passing the blame.)

Make a reasonable boundary and reasonable rules and keep them. Tell the players the name of the game and that you are not playing. They know the rules. You know the rules. If a rule is broken, apply consequences.

5 THE CONTROL AND POWER GAME

A game of power and control. It can appear like a real friendly game. It just gets defensive or mean if you don't play.

6 THE DOOR MAT GAME

"You are nothing but dirt under my feet." The victim becomes a person without rights, one only to be directed or walked on by another. A twist to this game is the martyr game where the victim becomes a martyr thinking they are doing this all for the right reasons or for God.

OTHER GAMES

THE GAME OF BROKEN COVENANT

This game divides: covenant, home, children, family and money. The lie that is believed: "No harm to live in sexual relationships outside of marriage". Marriage really isn't sacred. There are no responsibilities, no commitment, it is okay to throw away the child. Abortion is okay. Sexual relationships have become a covenant-breaking game with no rules.

THE NO COPE GAME

Suicide is a game sometimes played by self to hurt others. It can be found in, feeling sorry for "poor me", or in a lost of all hope for a future. This self-pity game can lead to an ultimate act of mental or physical suicide. Another way to play this game is the game of elimination: drive-by shootings, random violence, assisted suicide. Society is beginning to play all of the above.

THE MIND GAME

You make up your own game to include the following: worship/ power/authority/philosophy. You make up rules as you go. It is lawlessness as a game.

THE NAME GAME

This is a game of ownership. The game uses semantics to achieve the desired result. Call abortion, "pro-choice" so that abortion sounds like freedom of choice to the unknowing. Call the baby a "fetus to take away the baby's status and the baby's rights as a human being. Call homosexuals "gay" to twist the original intent of the term gay, and also to make it appear as if homosexuality is a happy life style. Call Conservatives "right-wing radicals". Call removing porn from school libraries "book burning" or loss of the first amendment rights. Call lying "moral relativism" or "situational ethics". If the term does not work change the term.

But what about how your own name can be used carelessly? God knew who you were to become and when you were born, your name reflected the meaning and purpose for your life. However, just as with colors and numbers,names can carry negative meanings. So we see a name can reflect life, a future hope in God or reflect nothing (total void, emptiness).

For example, a child is slow at completing tasks. Someone might start to call him Slow Joe. Everyone might think this is funny at the time. The child may even respond and the child starts to move slowly and think of himself as slow.

His name means wisdom. This is how God views Joe even if Joe's present circumstances appear differently God sees a finished product. He gave Joe a name containing life! His name means he has understanding and wisdom.

Names can give forth life or death. For example, hemlock can be a beautiful, green tree providing shade and life or it can be a poison administering death. Once I prayed for a street named Hemlock to change its nature to a growing, prospering street. Amazing events happened on that street after prayer. It began to prosper!

We have looked at negative games in the ways people relate; they don't even realize they are gaming. Now let's take a look at sugggesions on how to build positive relationships.

POSITIVE RELATIONSHIPS

Scriptures contain great advice for maintaining positive relationships. As with much in God's Kingdom, maintaining healthy relationships is a choice. Sometimes one person does not make the right choices in a relationship and the relationship ends. Still, on our part we can make the decision to forgive, be healed and go forward. Positive choices get easier as you practice them. The choice is always to love and always to forgive.

In relationships there will always be difficulties. Sometimes it is little things that continue to be irritating or big things where hurt seems overwhelming. Some issues are due to the way we were raised, some a matter of thoughtlessness and selfishness. Remember, we are all creatures that fall short, and God forgives our sin only as we forgive others.

The Bible directs us to consider the log in our own eye before we take the speck out of our brother's eye. Our own faults are so close to us they are impossible for us to see. It is so much easier to point out the fault of others.

God wants us to deal with self first, not concentrate on our brother's faults. We can do this by going to the Father and asking him to reveal our faults, hidden motivations, sins, actions and unhealthy patterns of behavior and unhealthy desires bound up in our own hearts. Where is it we need healing or are holding hurt and unforgiveness? We need to address outward actions and the hidden motivations that cause our outward responses. Only then can we deal (in kindness) with the faults of others.

Yes, we must deal with others through forgiveness, but to blindly avoid or never address or openly discuss issues is not the answer. When we do address issues here are some positive, problem-solving skills.

Positive Problem Solving Guidelines

1. <u>Set aside a quiet Place to Share</u>

2. <u>Always Stick to the Issue at Hand</u>

3. Observe Verbal and Non-Verbal Communication
Avoid using: you always or you never, name calling, swearing, false accucations, stomping, slamming things, or physically hurting people. Own up to your own poor behavior choices. Be observant of body language: crossing arms, legs or avoiding eye contact means that person is not agreeing. Know different cultures express different body languages.

4. Resolve Issues in Private
Avoid public humiliation, being overly critical or nagging. Don't make small things an issue; resolve them yourself.

5. Be Liberal in Kindness
Know praise is often a much faster way to change an an attitude. Respect each other, speak hope, love and generous amounts of forgiveness and kindness.

6. Pray ! Recognize the Real Enemy (2 Cor 10:4)
I demolish arguments and every pretension that sets sets itself up against the knowledge of God, and I take captive every thought to make it obedient to Christ!

REVIEW AND APPLICATION

The Glory - Christian Primary II presents the language of the Kingdom of God found through knowing Jesus, the Son of God, the King of Glory. Through color you came to understand the language spoken, to speak that language, to walk in the anointing of king, priest and prophet and to understand positive order and relationship.

Color, voice and number define (enlarge the understanding) of the Language of God. Now you can discern the light you see, listen for the voice you hear (spoken or written), or observe through relationship what language is being spoken.

References

The following are Scripture references related to light, and the color contained in light. Each positive definition represents a portion of God's covenant. We begin with an overview of references for the Glory. I would like to acknowledge Teresa Wilson for her assistance with the research on many of the Scripture references listed below.

King David concludes his final Psalm (Psalm 72:19) proclaiming, "*May the whole world be filled with Glory of God.*"

Planet Earth - Covenant of Glory	Genesis 9:12-17
Jesus - The King of Glory	Psalm 24:7-10
Rainbow - Glory of the Lord	Ezekiel 1:28
Counterfeit Glory	Revelation 9:17

LIGHT

Angels and light	Acts 12:7
Arise and shine	Isaiah 60:1
Be full of light	Matthew 6:22
Become sons of light	John 12:36
Children of light	Ephesians 5:8
Countenance of God	Psalm: 89:15
Everlasting light	Isaiah 60:19
Fruit of light	Ephesians 6:9
Giving light to the eyes	Psalm 19:8
Glory of the Lord	Revelation 22:6
God is light	I John 1:5
God is the light of life	Psalm 56:13
God made us a light	Acts 13:47
Gospel is light	2 Corinthians 4:4
Jesus is the light	John 3:16, 8:12, 9:5
Just rule	2 Samuel 23:1-4

Life	John 1:4
Light around us	Acts 26:13
Light for the Gentiles	Isaiah 42:6
Lord turns darkness into light	2 Samuel 22:29
No darkness in light	John 1:5-10, 2:9-11
Our armor of light	Romans 13:12
Path and life	Job 24:13, 27:28
	Proverbs 4:18
	Isaiah 2:5 Psalms 56:13
Satan masquerades	2 Corinthians 11:14
Sons of the light	1 Thessolanians 5:5
The Lord is my light	Psalm 27:1
The Word of God	Psalm 119:105
To rule	Genesis 1:15-16
You are light	Matthew 5:14-16
Walk in the light	Isaiah 2:5
We are Light in darkness	Romans 2:19
We are light to nations	Isaiah 42:6

WHITE

Angel's garment	Deuteronomy 28:3
Bride	Revelation 19:7-8
Conqueror	Revelation 6:2, 2:17
Glory, glorified	Mark 9:3, Matt 17:2
Glorified Christ	Revelation 1:14
Heavenly garment	Revelation 4:4, 7:8
Purity	Isaiah 1:18
Righteous - washed clean	Revelation 7:13-15
To overcome	Revelation 3:5, 2:17

YELLOW/GOLD

Authority	Revelation 14:14
Belonging to the Lord	Haggai 2:8, I Kings 1:20
Gold, richness	Genesis 13:2
Blessing	Genesis 24:35
Crown	Revelation 4:4
Disease	Leviticus 13:30
False foundation	Corinthians 3:12
False worship (Idols)	Exodus 32:31, 32:4,
	Revelation 9:20
Golden prayers	Revelation 5:8
Lord to be more desired	Psalm 19:10
Offering	Exodus 28:36-38
Satanic army	Revelation 9:17
Stone in breastplate	Ezekiel 8:2 (Jasper)
Temple of the Lord	Exodus 25- Numbers 8
Worship	Matthew 2:1

RED

Blood - protection	Exodus 12:7, 13
(redemption)	Leviticus 16:14,
	Matthew26:28,
	Exodus 30:10
Breastplate of priest	Revelation 4:3
Cleansing	Hebrews 9:14
Forgiveness, atonement	Numbers 19:1-4,
	Hebrews 9 :14
Satanic army	Revelation 9:17
Sin	Isaiah 1:18
The Dragon	Revelation 12:3
Vengeance, redemption	Isaiah 63:1-6,
	Revelation 1:5-6

War, fire	Revelation 9:14-19
Warfare/blood	Revelation 6:4,
	Naham 2:3, Kings 3:22

BLUE

Counterfeit	Revelation 9:17
Garment, royalty	Ester 8:15
Heaven	Exodus 24:10,10:1
Priestly	Exodus 28:5-8
Remembrance	Numbers 15:38, 40
Throne of God	Ezekiel 1:26
To wrap (Holy Spirit)	Numbers 4:6-12

ORANGE

Orange is not directly referred to in the Bible.

GREEN

Life, Living plants, trees	Genesis 1:30, 9:3
	Joel 2:22
Peace	Psalm 23:2
Righteous, Covenant	Revelation 4:3

PURPLE

Covering	Numbers 4:13
Garments of wealth	Proverbs 31:22
Kingship, robe of Jesus	Mark 15:17, 20
Promise land - land of purple	Exodus 25:4
	Joshua 2:2
Riches	Daniel 5:29, Ester 8:15
Royal robes	Judges 8:26,

BLACK

Before the coming of the Lord   Joel 2:31
Bridgroom   Matthew 25:1
Sickness   Job 30:26-31
     Revelation 6:5-8

NAMES AND TITLES IN COLOR

JESUS   SATAN

White/Light

The Light of the World   The Father of Lies
(John 8:12)   (John 8:43-44)

Gold/Yellow

Lion of the Tribe of Judah   The Roaring Lion
(Revelation 5:5)   (1 Peter 5:8)
     Day Star, Son of
     Dawn (Isaiah 14:12)

Red

The Lamb who takes away sin   The Red Dragon
(John 1:28)   (Revelation 12:3)
The Rose of Sharon (Solomon 2:1)

Blue

The Prince of Peace   Prince of the Power of
(Isaiah 9:6)   the Air (Ephesians 2:2)

Green

The True Vine   Foul spirits like frogs
(John 15:1) Savior   (Revelation 16:13)
Redeemer   Vine of the earth
     (Revelation 14:18,19)

<u>Orange</u>

The Mighty Counselor	The false prophet
(Isaiah 9:6)	(Revelation 13:11)

<u>Purple</u>

A man of sorrows (Isaiah 53:3)	Great prostitute
The King of the Jews	(Revelation 17:1-4)
(Mark 15:17) King of Kings	

<u>Brown</u>

The last Adam	The Beast
(I Corinthians 15:45-46)	(Revelation Chapter 13)

<u>Black</u>

The Bridegroom (Mark 2:18-19)	The antichrist
Holder of keys to death/hades	(1 John 4:2-3)
(Revelation 1:18)	Death (Revelation 6:8),
	(Hebrews 2:14)

JESUS IN NUMBERS

In the beginning was the Word. Through Him all things were made; without Him nothing was made that has been made (John 1:3). He is the Light of the World.

This Holy One, anointed One, the One and only Son of God who was first and last became the first born son of Mary (1) and the first born from the dead. He is our new covenant (2). He is the One who is (3), our mediator and high priest who holds the office of king, priest and prophet (3) and is the second person of the triune God (3). He is the one who is, who was and who is to come. He is the way, the truth and the life (3).

He is the Savior of the world (4), crucified upon a cross (4) to take away the sins of the world (4). It was Jesus who gave the five-fold ministry (5) of apostles, prophets, evangelists, pastors and teachers to prepare God's people for service.

Now this Jesus sits at the right hand (5) of God the Father as the Lamb that is worthy to receive from the Father's right hand (5) the scroll of Revelation, chapter 5.

He is the Son of Man, the second Adam (6), Lord of the Sabbath (7) and the Lamb with seven horns and seven eyes (7). He is the one who walks among the seven lamp stands and holds the seven stars (7) in His right hand. He is our Alpha and Omega (8). After His resurrection Jesus revealed Himself to the disciples in 153 fish (9) and sent the Holy Spirit to those waiting in Jerusalem at nine o' clock in the morning (9).

SATAN IN NUMBERS

Satan is father of nothing but the lie. He was the one who led the rebellion in heaven with one-third of the angels of heaven following. He is the deceiver who undertook to alienate God from man and divides the brothers (2). He is the number of division. He is the beast (false prophet) from the book of Revelation that has two horns like a lamb (2) but speaks like a dragon and the three (3) evil spirits that look like frogs that come out of the mouth of the three (3) leaders of the final rebellion against God: the dragon, the beast and the false prophet.

He is the leader of the principalities, powers and rulers in high places (3) who was thrown to earth (4), represented as a serpent cursed to eat the dust of the earth.

Satan is the King of the Abyss and Lord of the Flies, the false prophet in the Book of Revelation who forces everyone great and small, rich and poor, free and slave to receive a mark on his right hand (5) or on his forehead, the mark of the beast (666).

And he is the leader and personification of destruction, the beast with seven horns, ten heads and ten crowns (7), who sits upon the city of seven (7) hills. With him there is no end but Hades, no hope, no future (8). He directs the nine (9) ruling spirits revealed in the text, *The Power.* He is the beast from chapter nine of Revelation.

The Name of Jesus in Color

Light/White: The Light, The Truth, the Man on the white horse in Revelation

Yellow: The Lion of the Tribe of Judah

Red: Redeemer, The Lamb that was slain

Blue: The Prince of Peace

Green: The Savior of the World

Orange: Prophet

Purple: The King of Kings, Suffering Servant

Brown: Son of Man

The Name of Jesus in Numbers

1 The Holy One
   The First, the Last, the One who is to come
2 Our Everlasting Covenant
3 Triune God Elohim (meaning three)
4 Emanuel (God with us) The Savior of the World
5 The Hand of God
6 The Second Adam

Spiritual Strength Training Series

THE KINGDOM - CHRISTIAN PRIMARY I $13.00

This study offers a comprehensive overview of God's Kingdom and Kingdom prayers. It includes basic Kingdom structure, practical applications of love, faith and hope, healing and inner healing.. 9x6 ISBN 0-9718325-0-1

The Kingdom Teacher's Manual $31.00

Developed by a veteran teacher, this easy-to-use teacher's guide to *The Kingdom* offers chapter study guidelines, 20 pages of hands-on activities, a treasure map and art of the four Gospels. 8 1/2 x 11 ISBN 0-9718325-3-6

The Revolution Begins - Kingdom Workbook $13.00

The Revolution Begins is the student workbook for participants in a study of *The Kingdom*. It contains journal sheets for dreams, visions and words from God. 8 1/2 x 11 ISBN 0-9718325-9-5

Wonderland -THE KINGDOM Music CD $10.00

THE GLORY - CHRISTIAN PRIMARY II $13.00

Jesus is the Glory and the Light of the World! Man was created to walk in the light of the His Glory. Here explore colors, numbers and the anointing of King, Priest and Prophet using color as a visual aid. 9x6 ISBN 0-9718325-1-X

The Glory Color Book- COLOR BOOK $ 10.00

Coloring pages to compliment *The Glory*. 8 1/2 x 11 ISBN 0-9718325-4-4

The Year of the Lyger -Powerpoint CD $13.00

Must have companion material for *The Glory*. The Lion and the Tiger release prophetic art for the king, priest and prophet. 8 1/2x11Lyger prints$30.00 each

THE POWER - CHRISTIAN PRIMARY III $13.00

The Power offers a practical guide to knowing the Holy Spirit and practicing deliverance. It reveals the gifts of the Holy Spirit, strageties for warfare and color charts the language the enemy speaks. 9x6 ISBN 0-9718325-2-8

The Sound of Deliverance $13.00

This CD is a powerpoint presentation of all prayers from the Spiritual Strength Training Series, plus more! ISBN 0-9718325-5-2

Rumors of Nard: The Book of 7, 8 and 9 $13.00

Powerpacked revelation of deliverance illustrated in allegory. The story reveals demonic forces found in *The Power*. 9X6 ISBN 0-9718325-7-9

Order Your Spiritual Strength Training Series Today!

Evensong Publishing,1934 Golfview Drive,Clarkston, Washington 99403
evensongpublishing.com *Cracking the Code for the 21st Century*

(503) 791-1922

.,

Evensong Publishing

Cracking the Code for the 21st Century

3811872

Made in the USA